color me horny

deena rae schoenfeldt

ISBN: 978-1542312271

ḅ

introduction

Long ago, in my misspent youth, I spent a lot of time in bars and honkytonks; some of the time I was even sober. I decided to take some of the lines I heard (and maybe a few I used), as well as ones my friends have heard, and do something useful with them ... I turned them into a coloring book.

Grab some colored pencils, a glass of your favorite drink, and sit down to enjoy some mindless "you" time without someone spilling their drink down your shirt or stepping on your toes.

Thanks!

Deena Rae

dedication

To Tiffany Fox, who encourages my shenanigans.

d

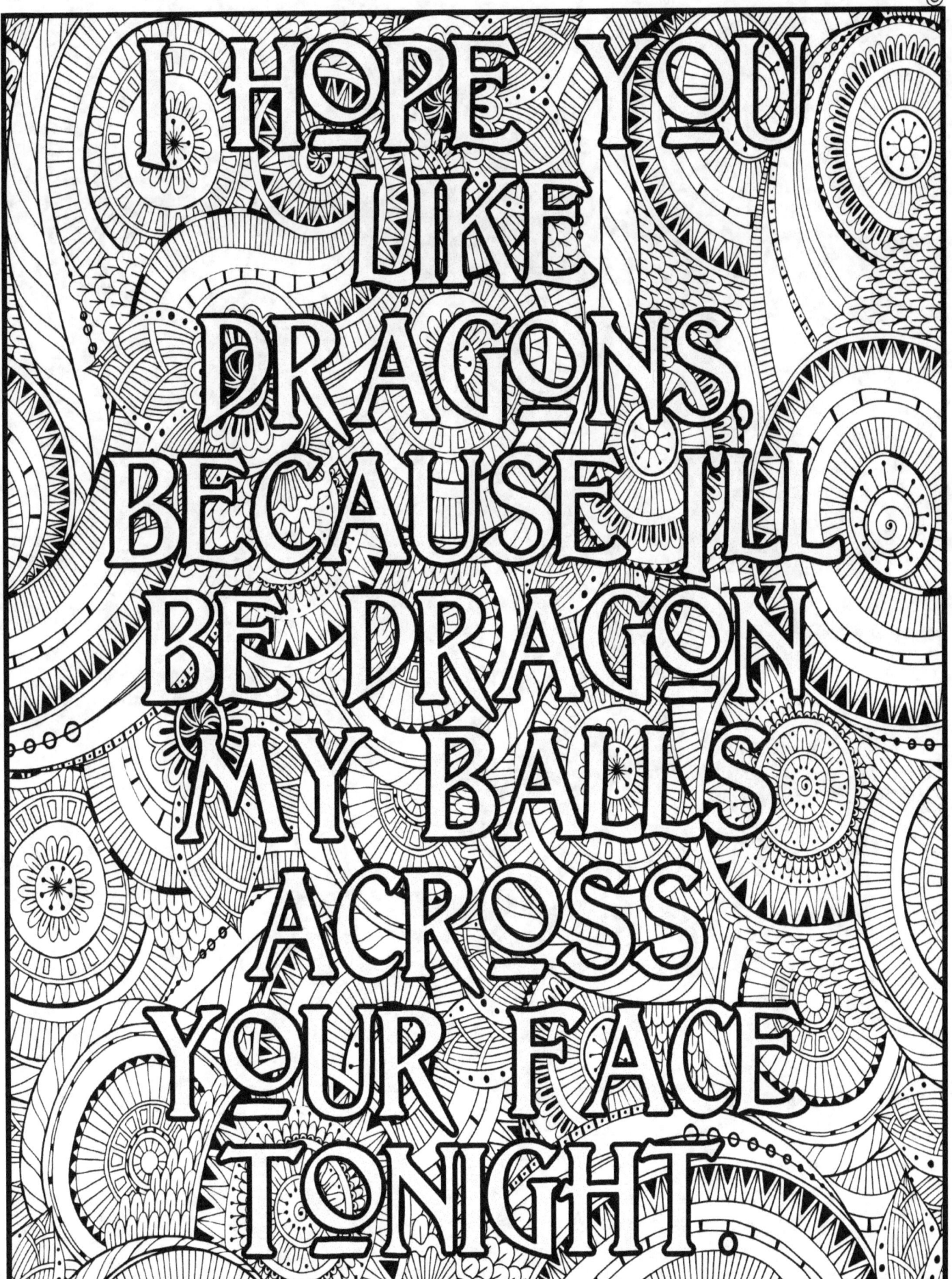

I HOPE YOU LIKE DRAGONS, BECAUSE I'LL BE DRAGON MY BALLS ACROSS YOUR FACE TONIGHT.

deena rae schoenfeldt

2

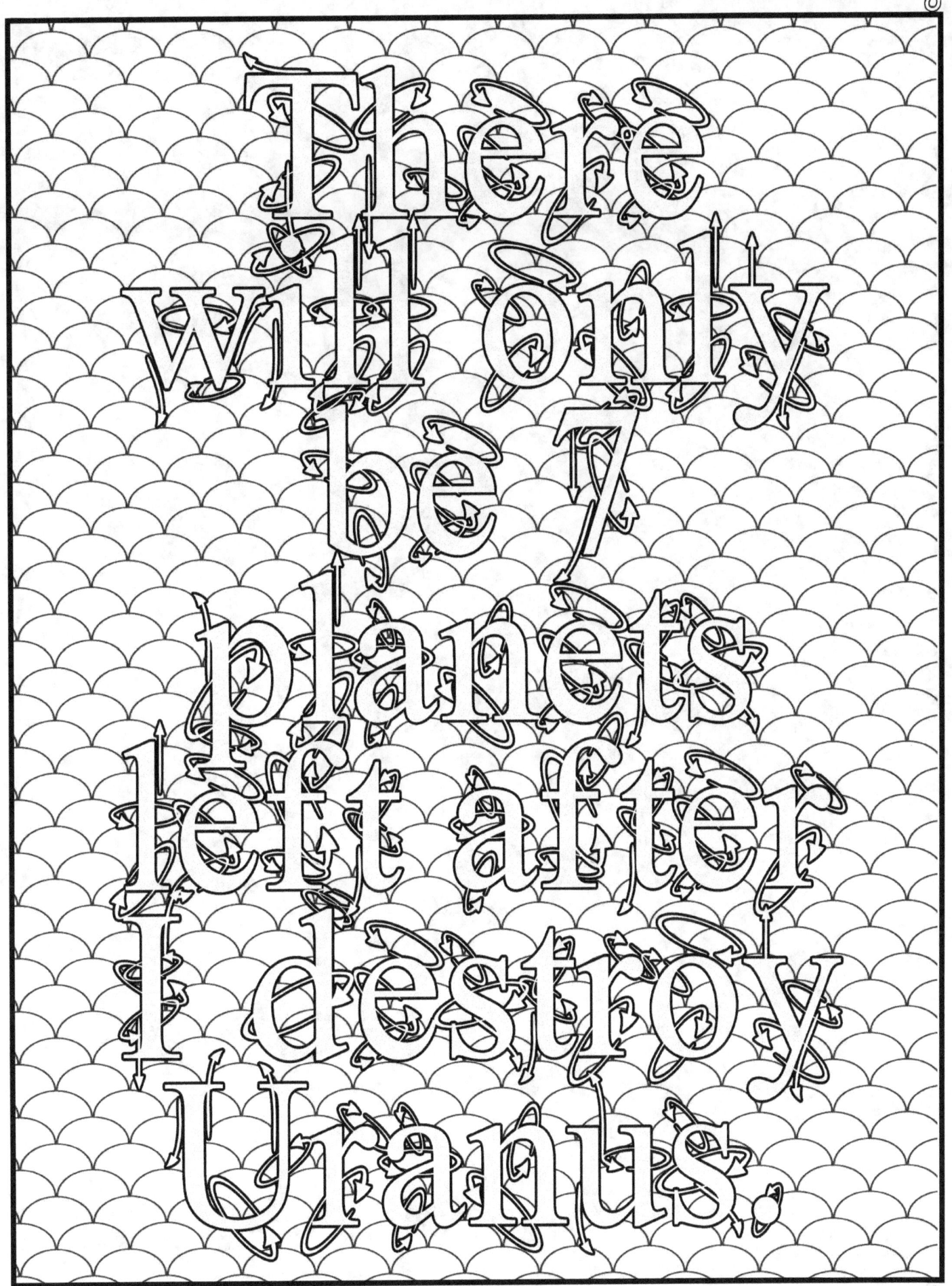

There will only be 7 planets left after I destroy Uranus.

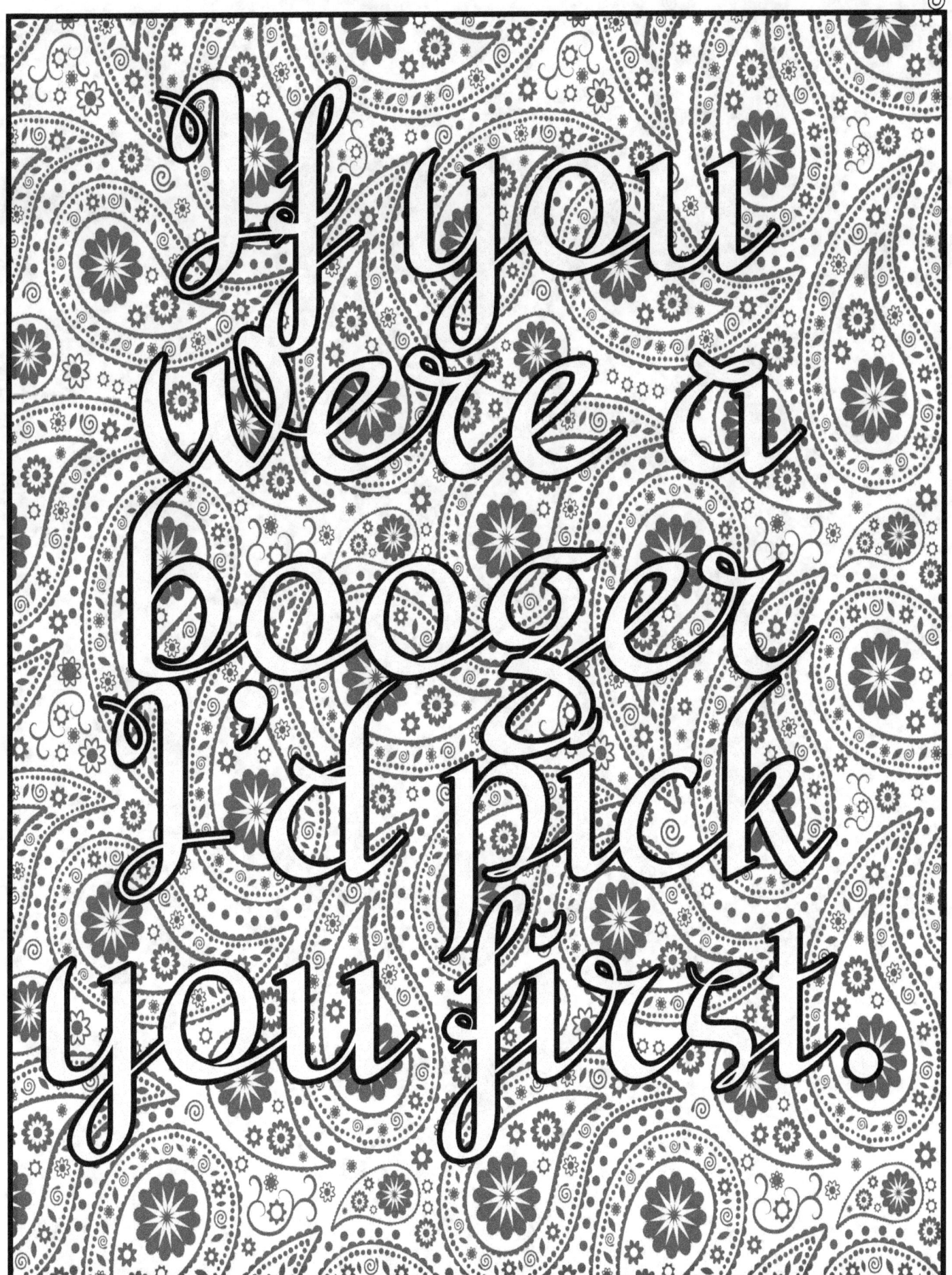

color me horny

If you were a booger I'd pick you first.

5

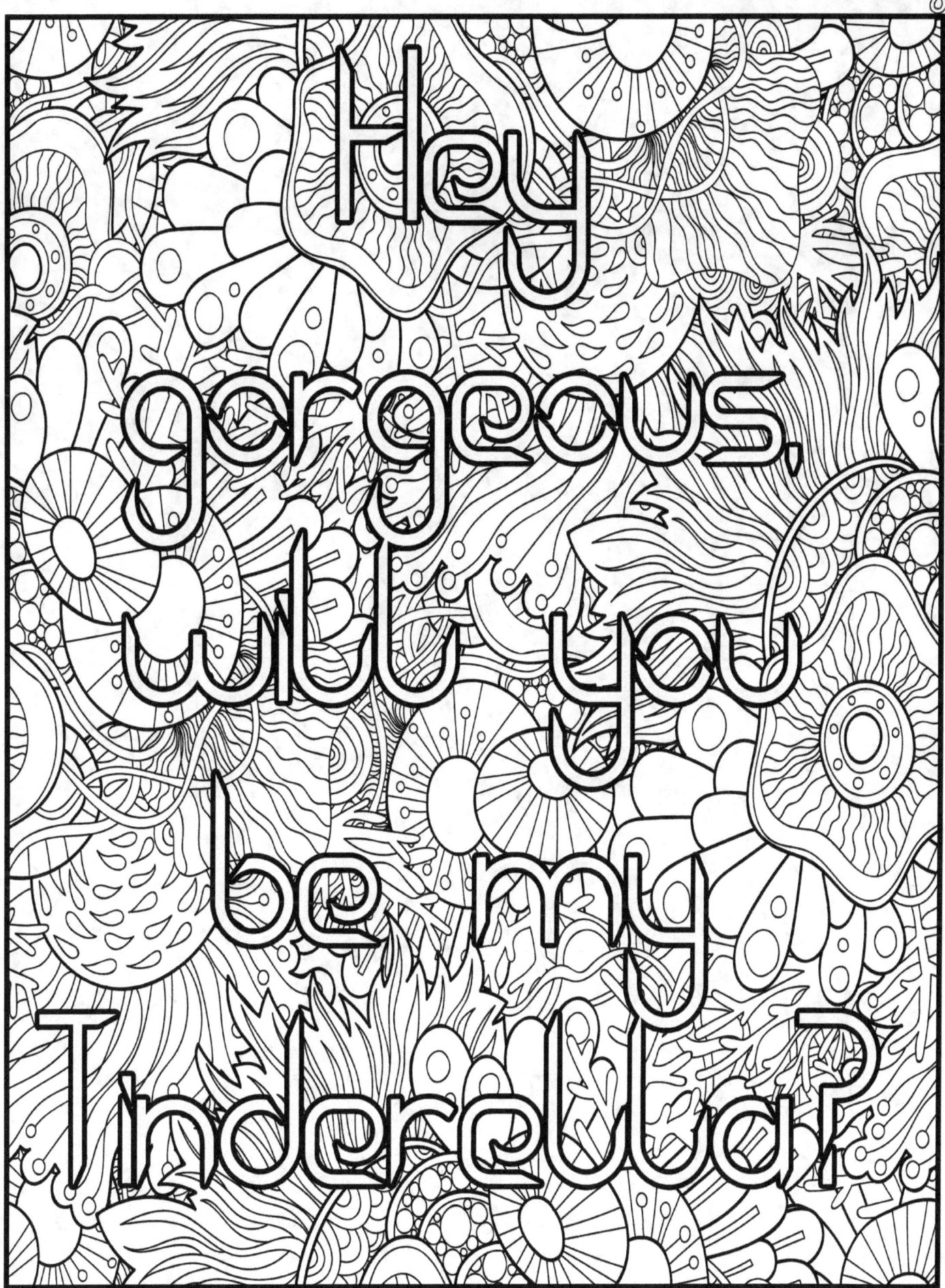

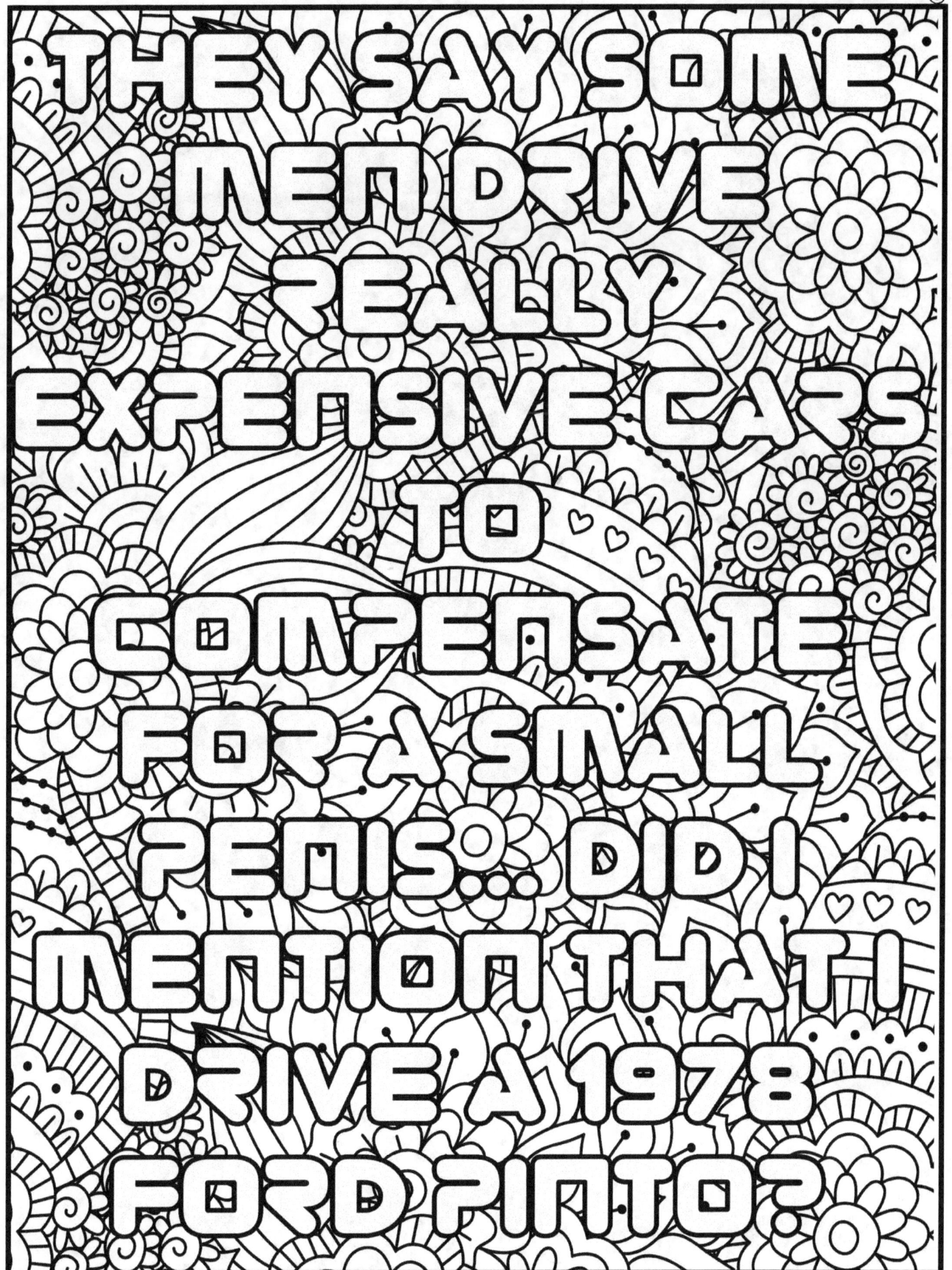

THEY SAY SOME MEN DRIVE REALLY EXPENSIVE CARS TO COMPENSATE FOR A SMALL PENIS... DID I MENTION THAT I DRIVE A 1978 FORD PINTO?

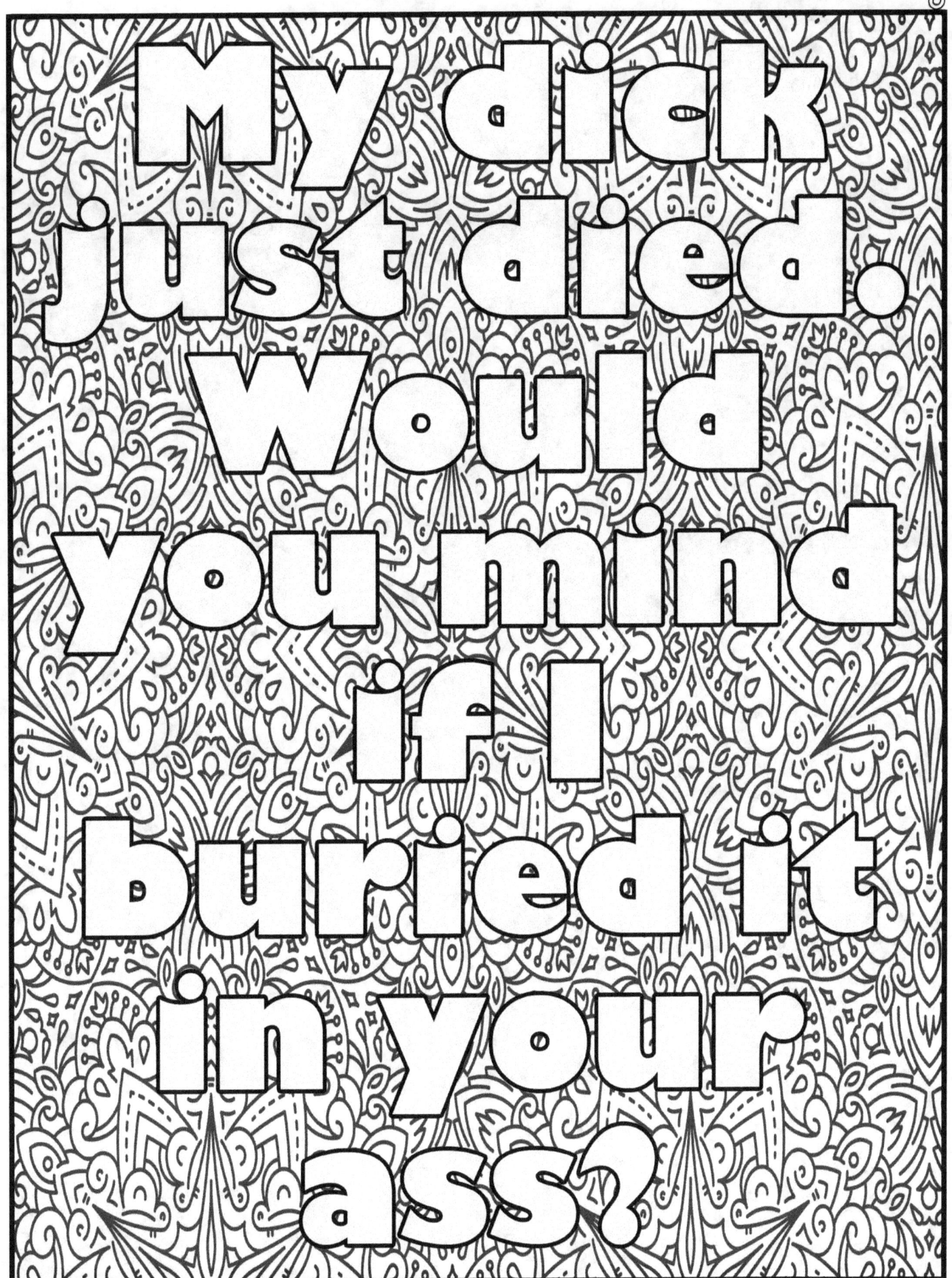

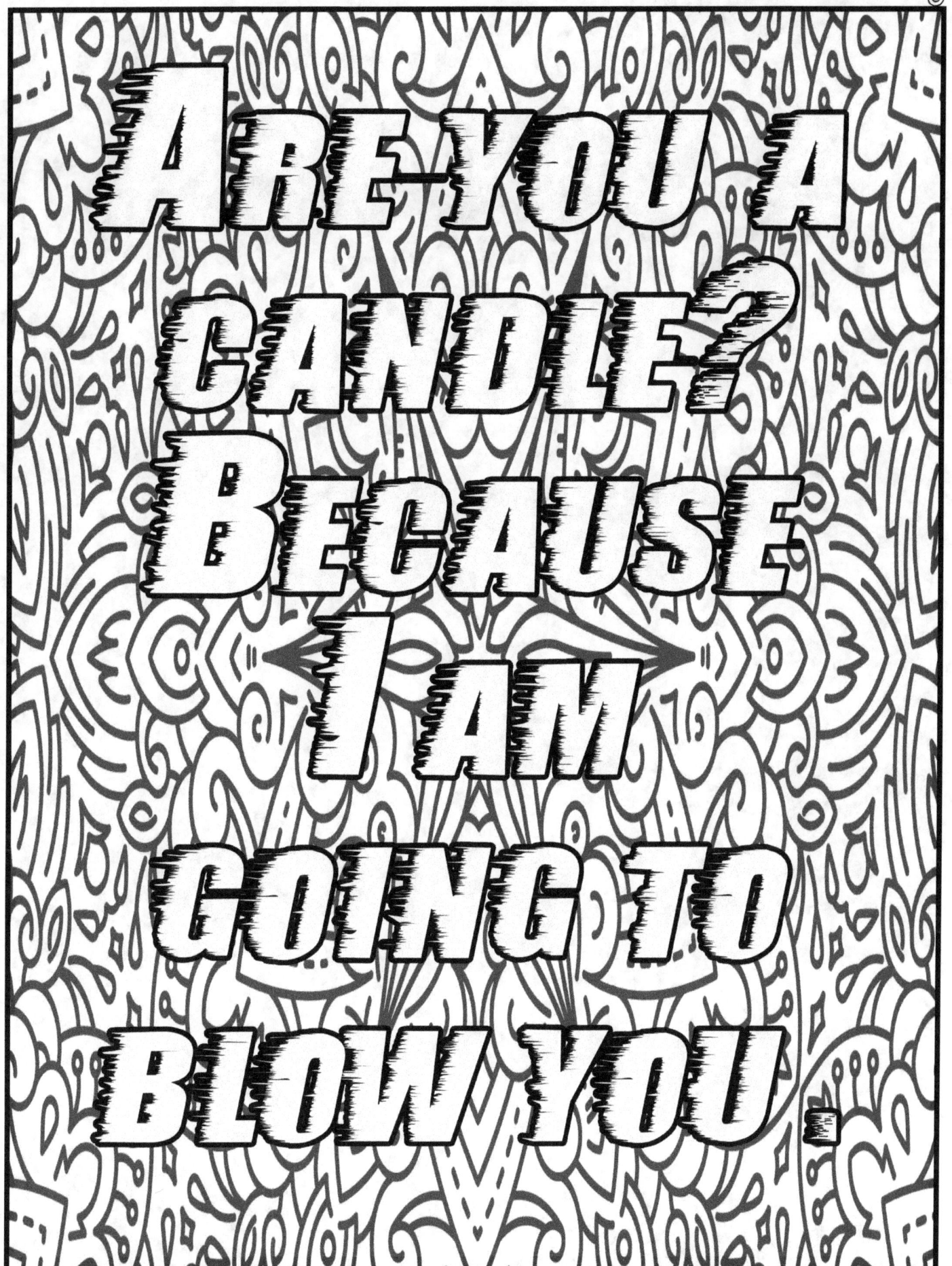

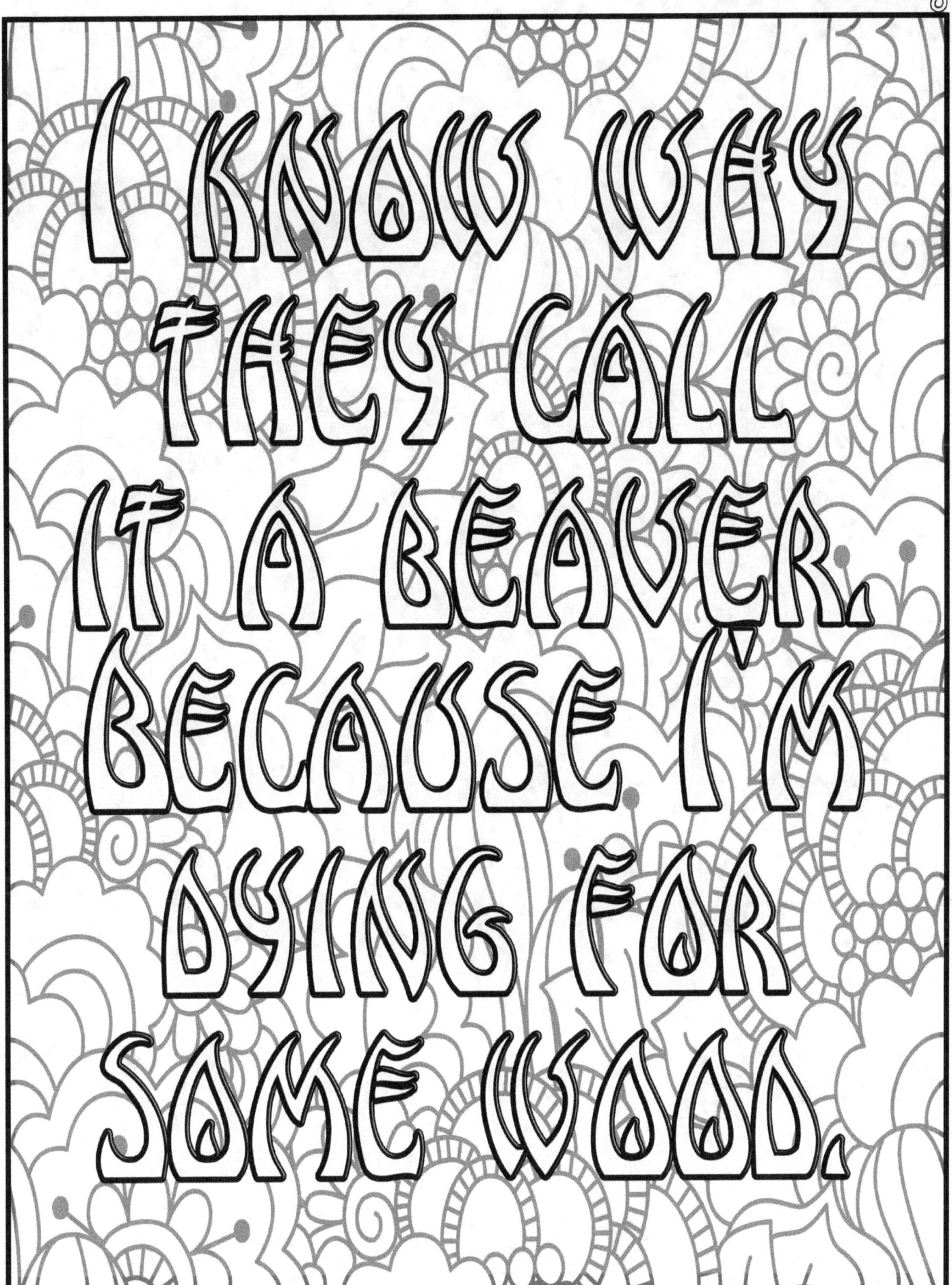

I KNOW WHY THEY CALL IT A BEAVER. BECAUSE I'M DYING FOR SOME WOOD.

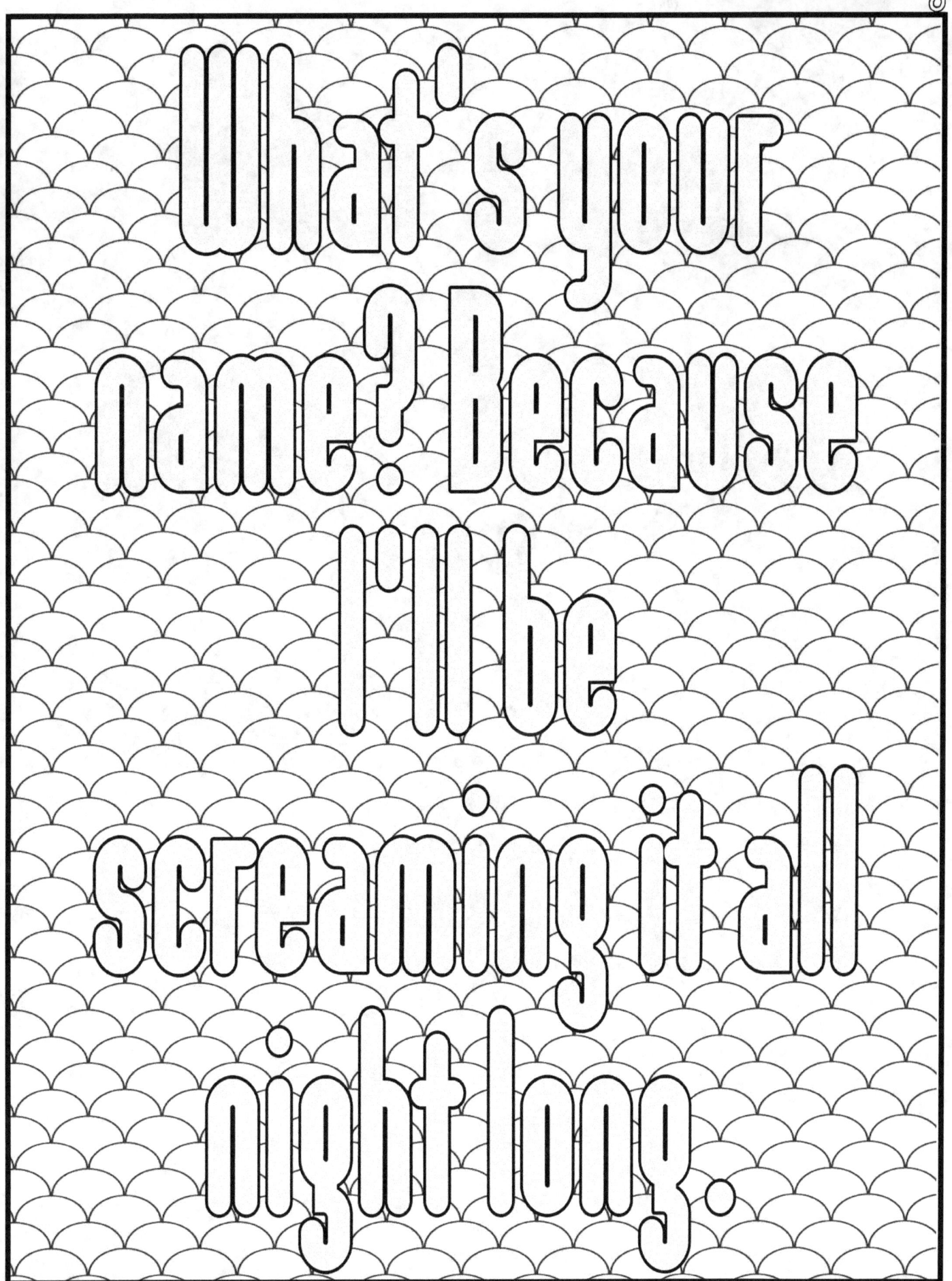

What's your name? Because I'll be screaming it all night long.

WANT TO GIVE ME AN AUSTRALIAN KISS? IT'S LIKE FRENCH KISSING, BUT YOU'RE GOING DOWN UNDER.

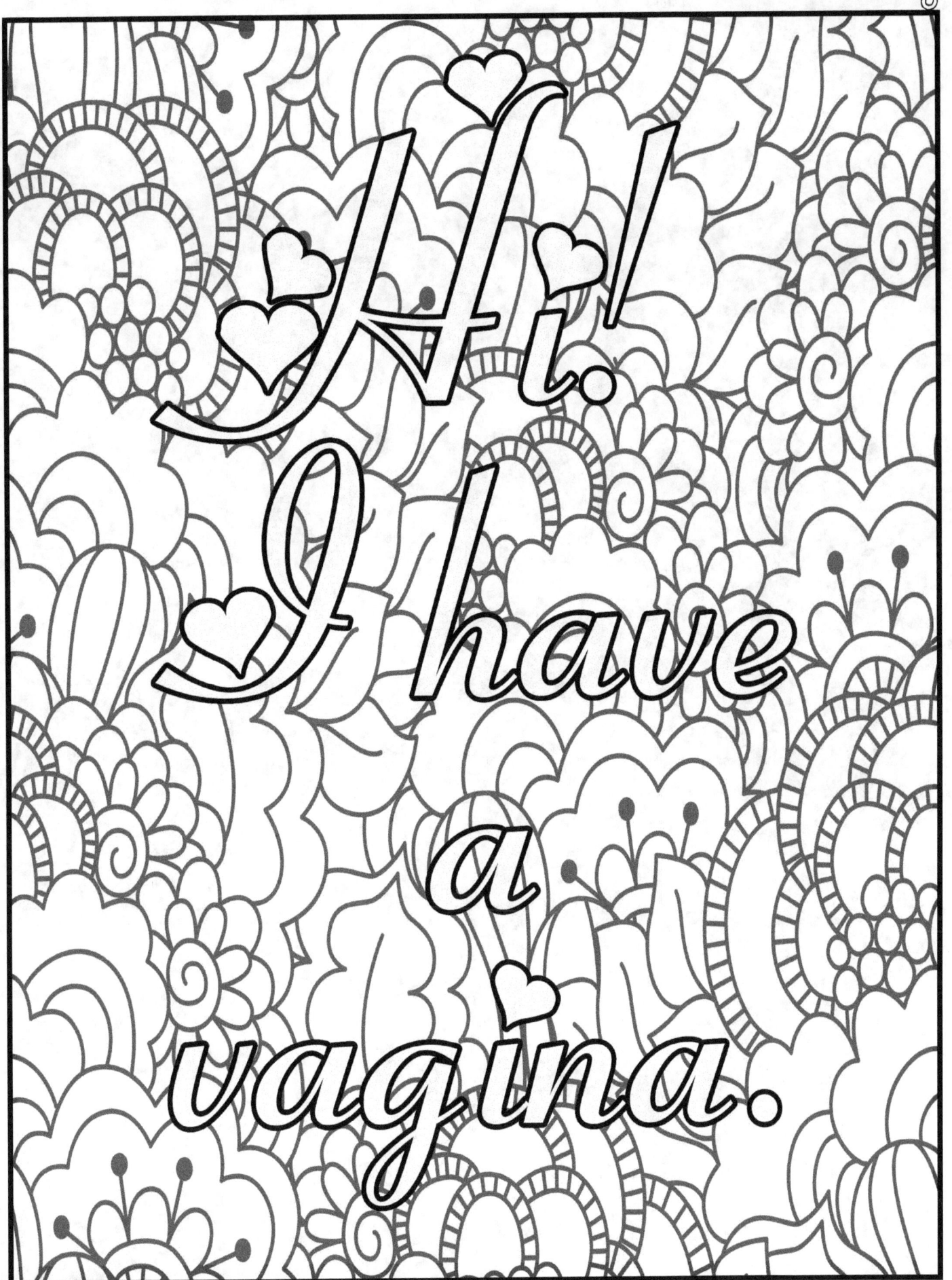

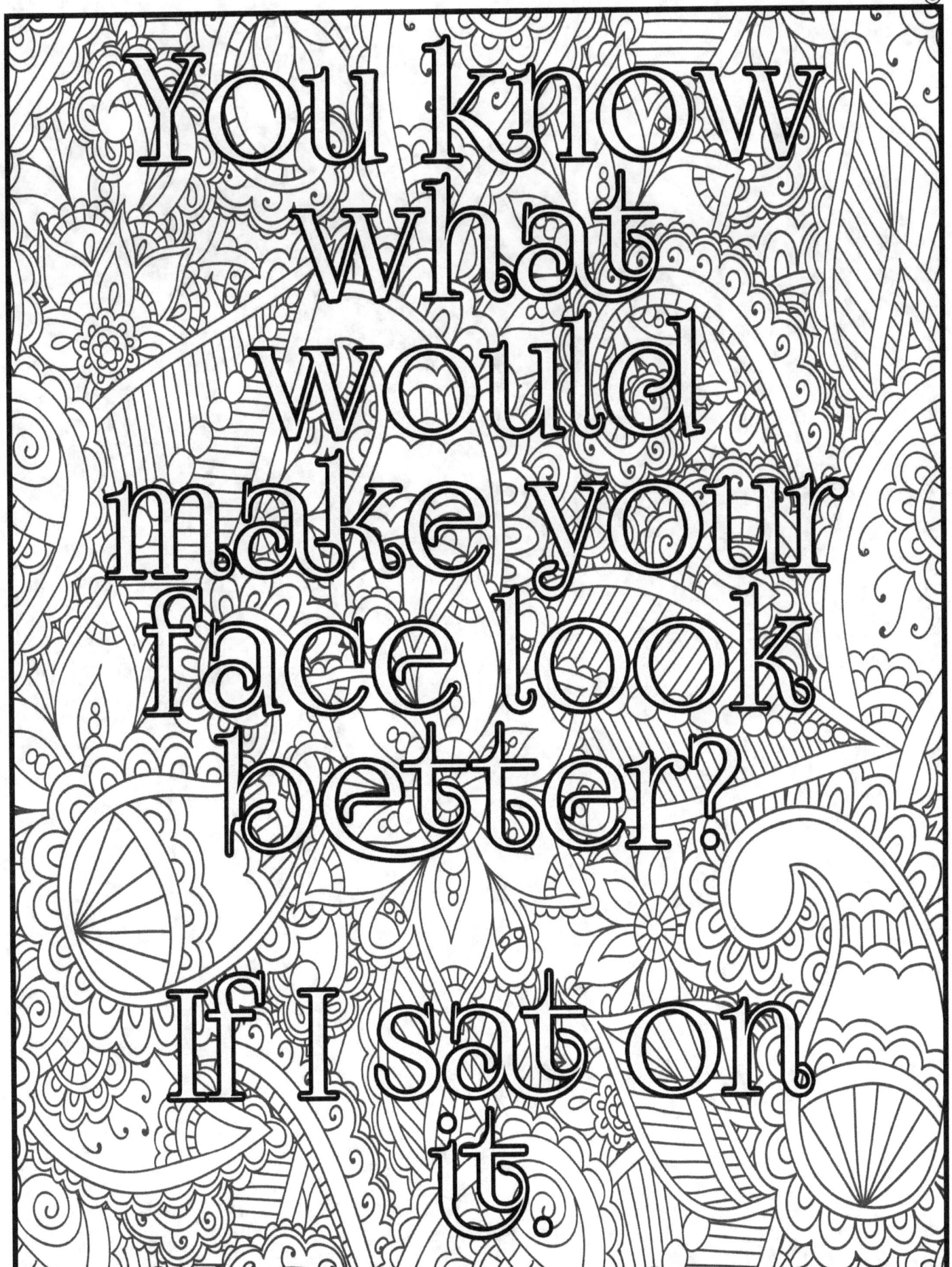

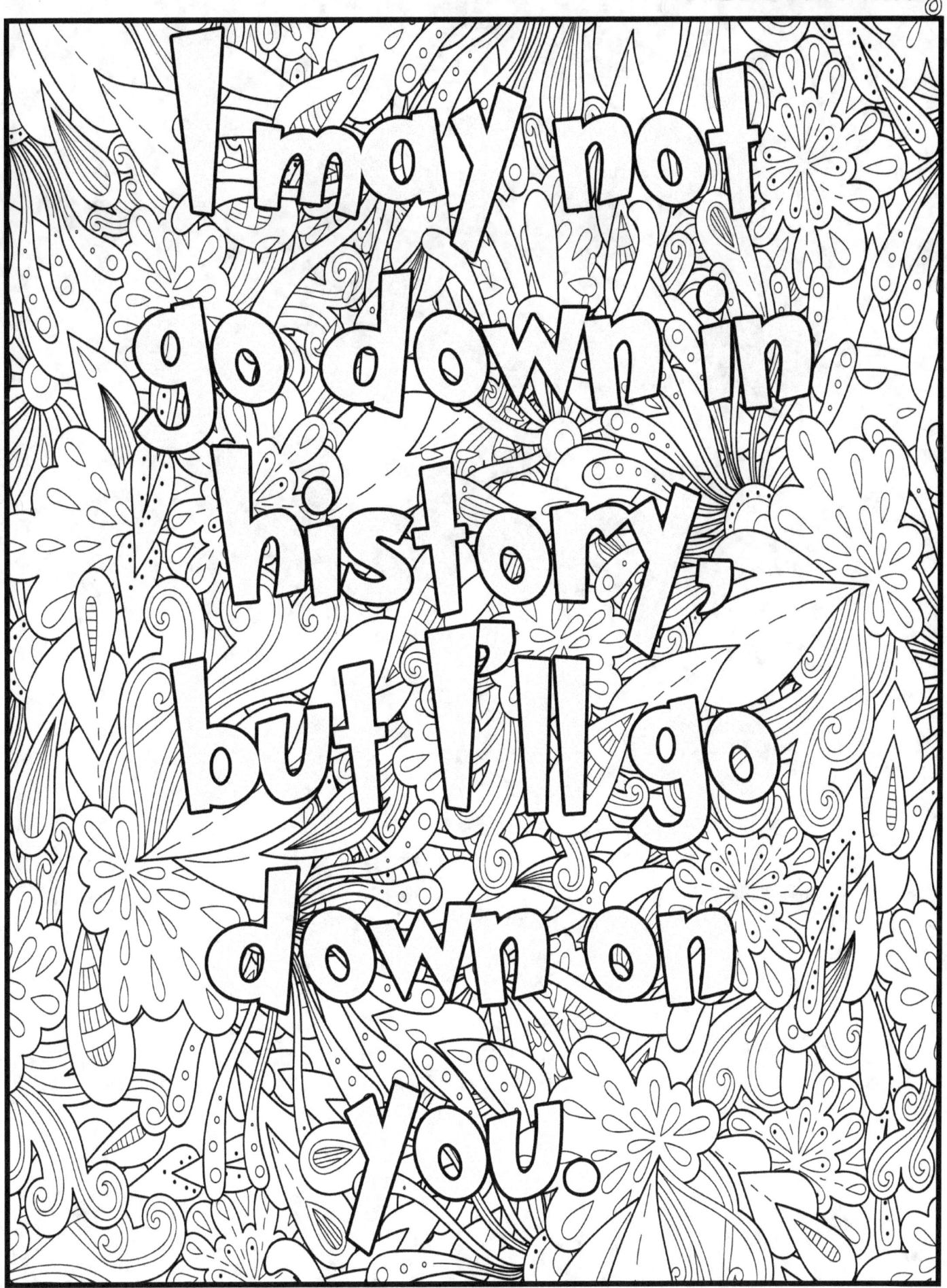

I may not go down in history, but I'll go down on you.

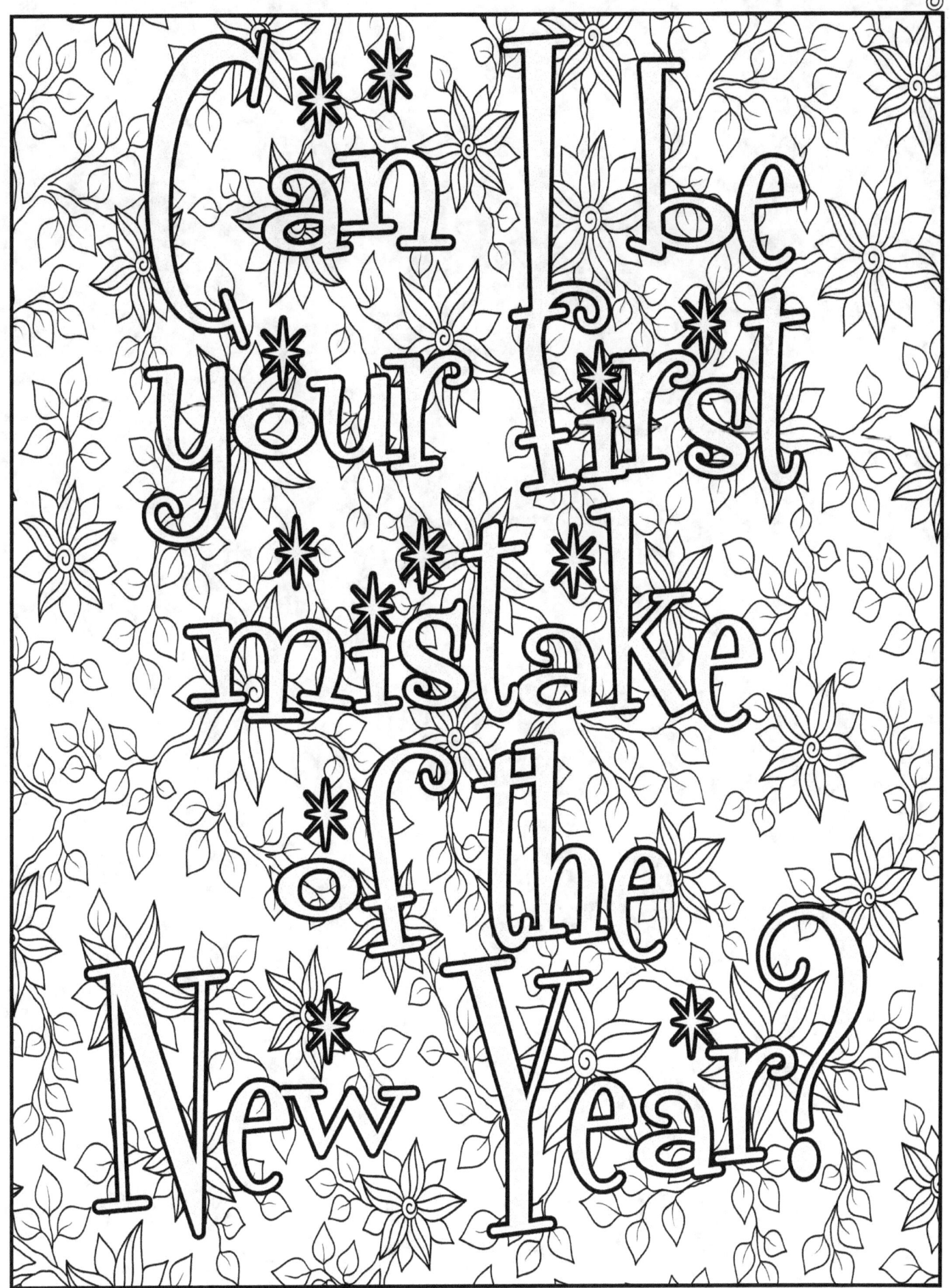

Can I be your first mistake of the New Year?

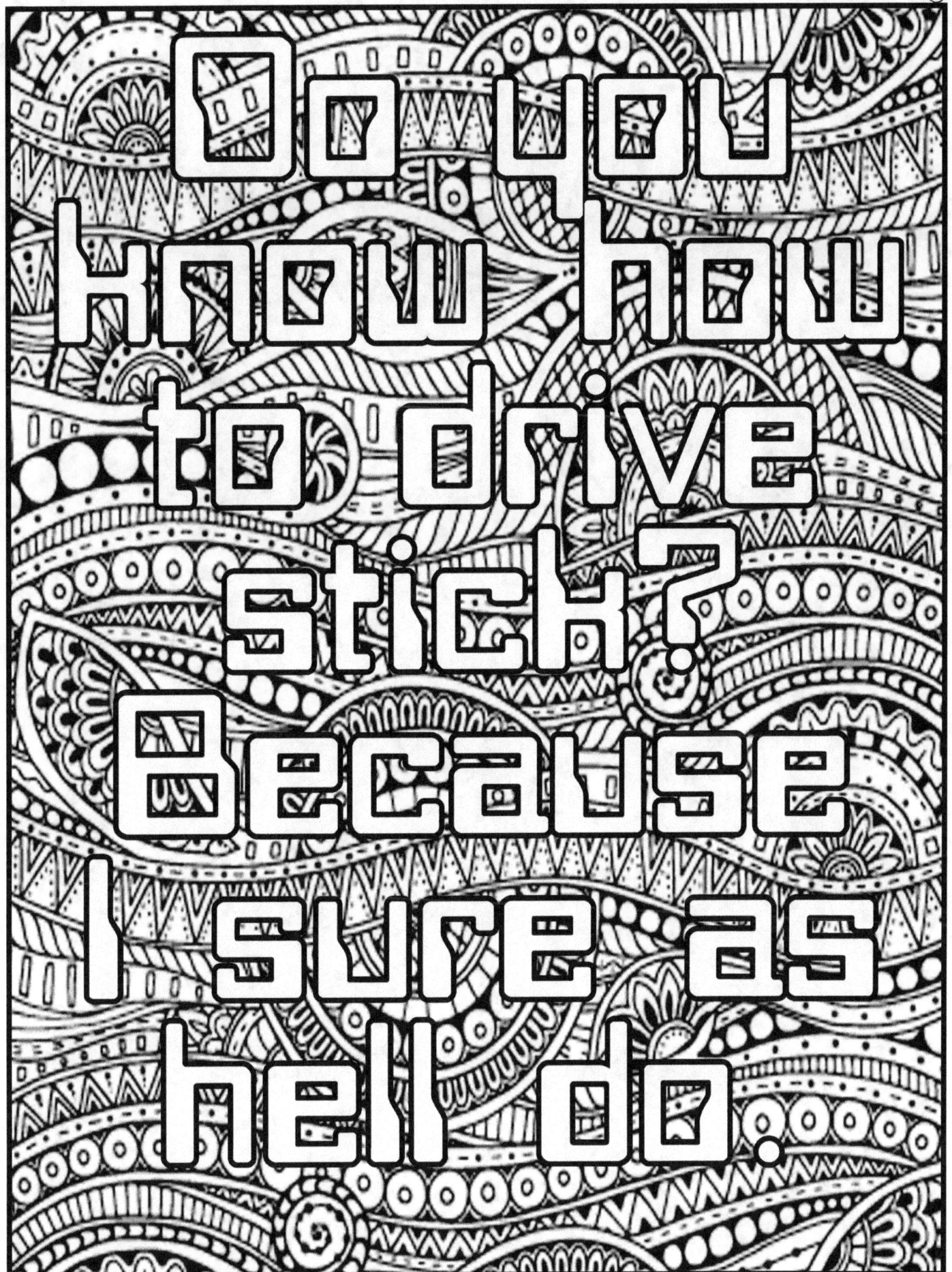

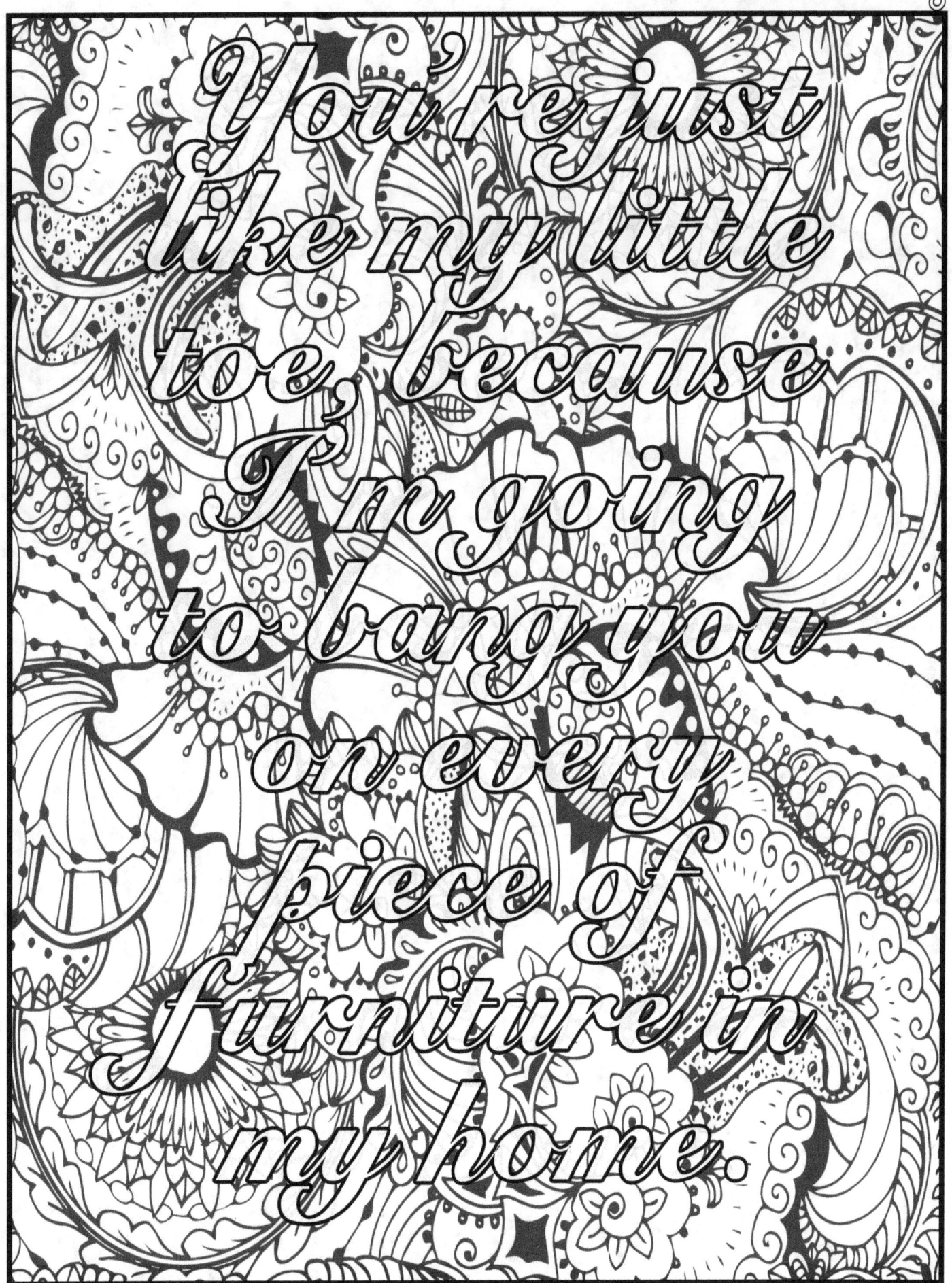

You're just like my little toe, because I'm going to bang you on every piece of furniture in my home.

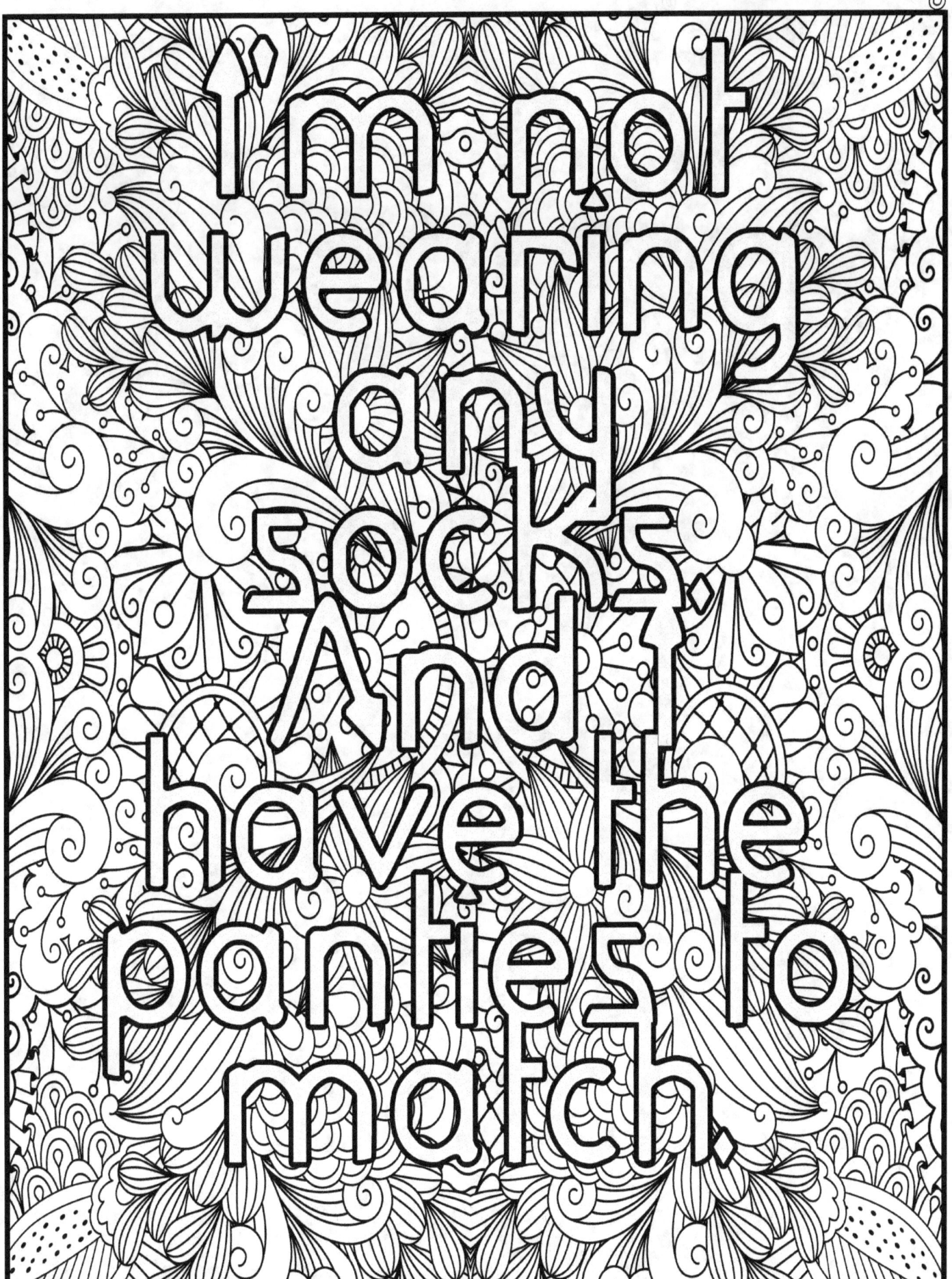

I'm not wearing any socks. And I have the panties to match.

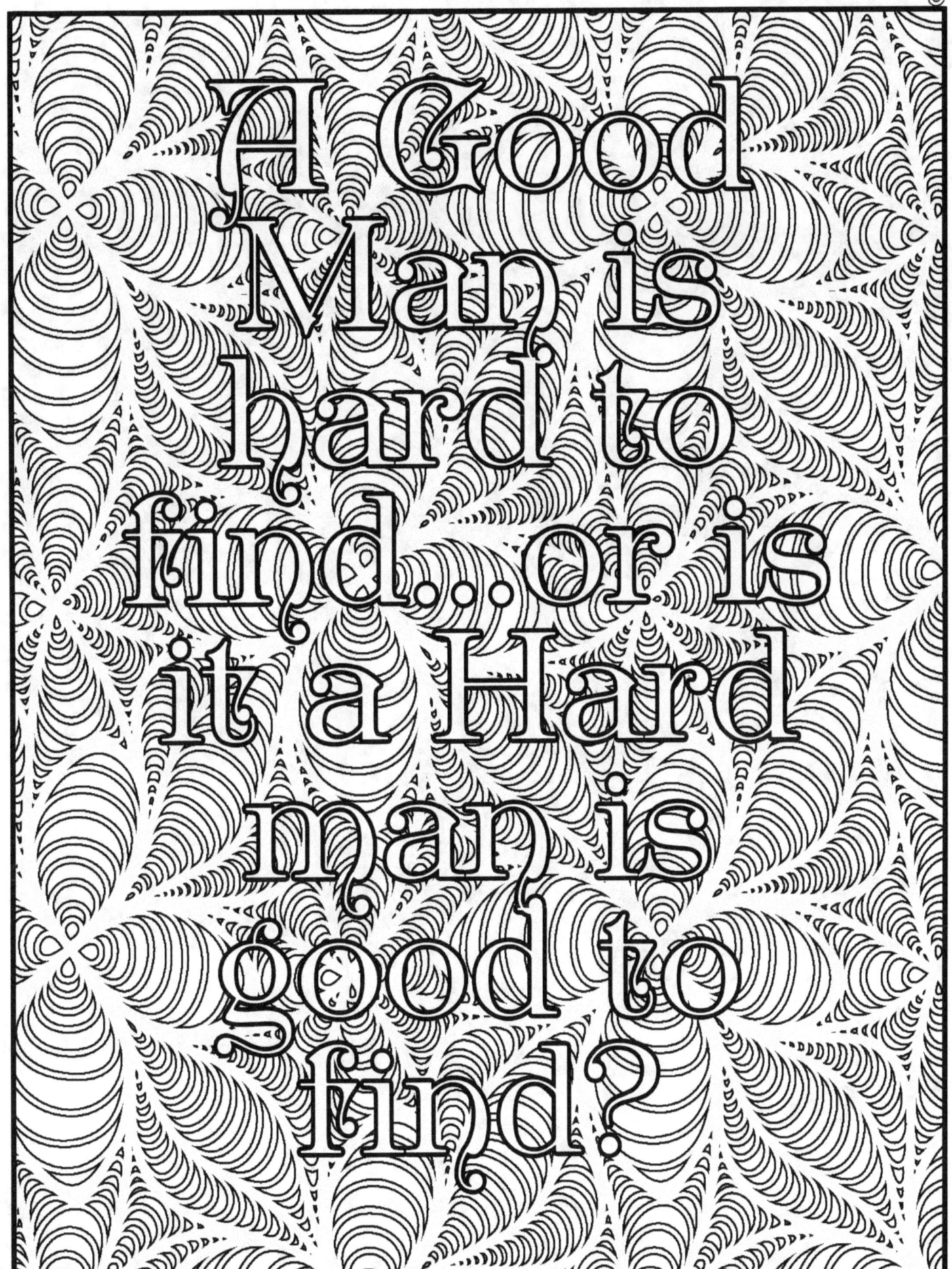

A Good Man is hard to find... or is it a Hard man is good to find?

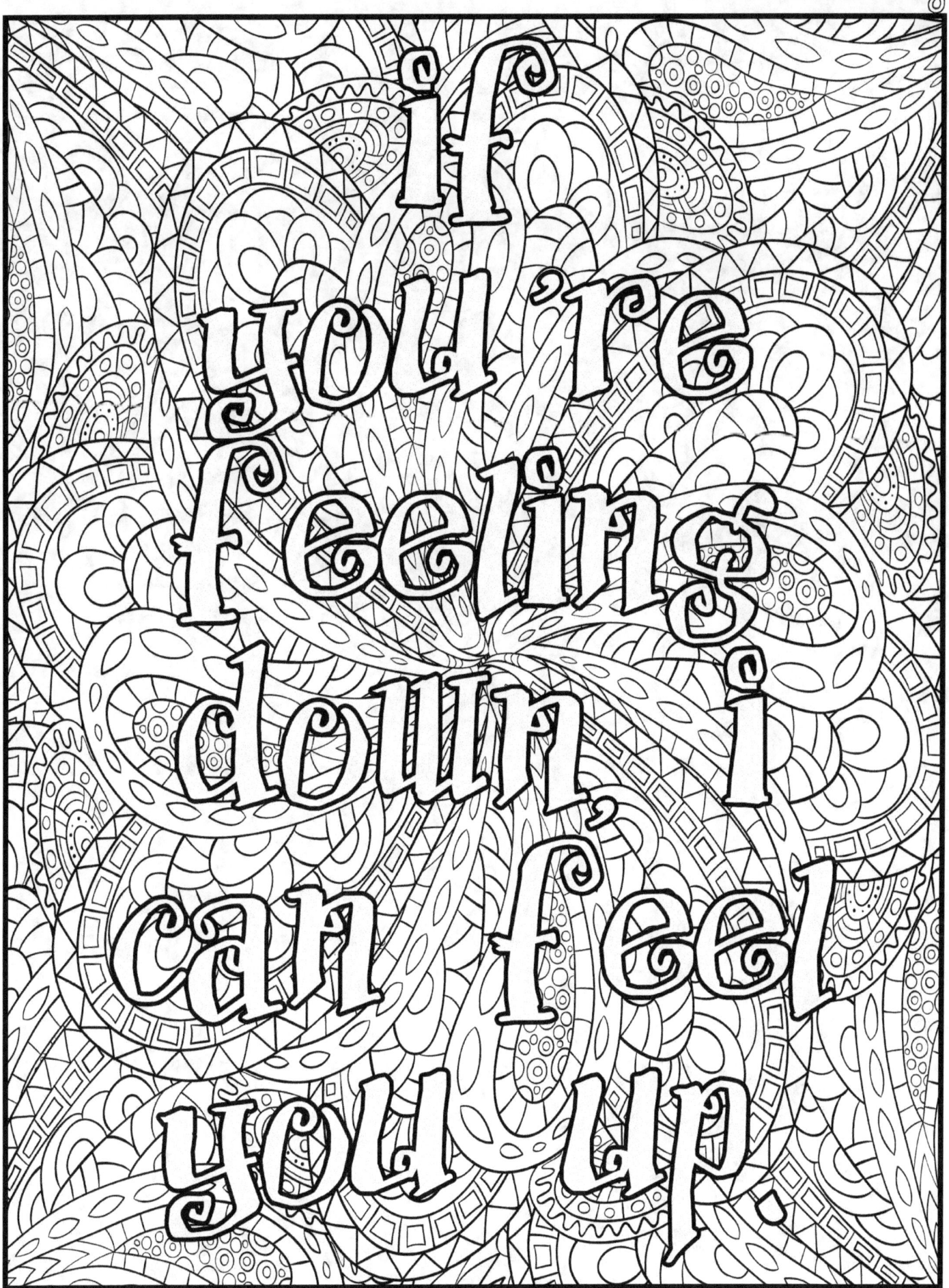

if you're feeling down, i can feel you up.

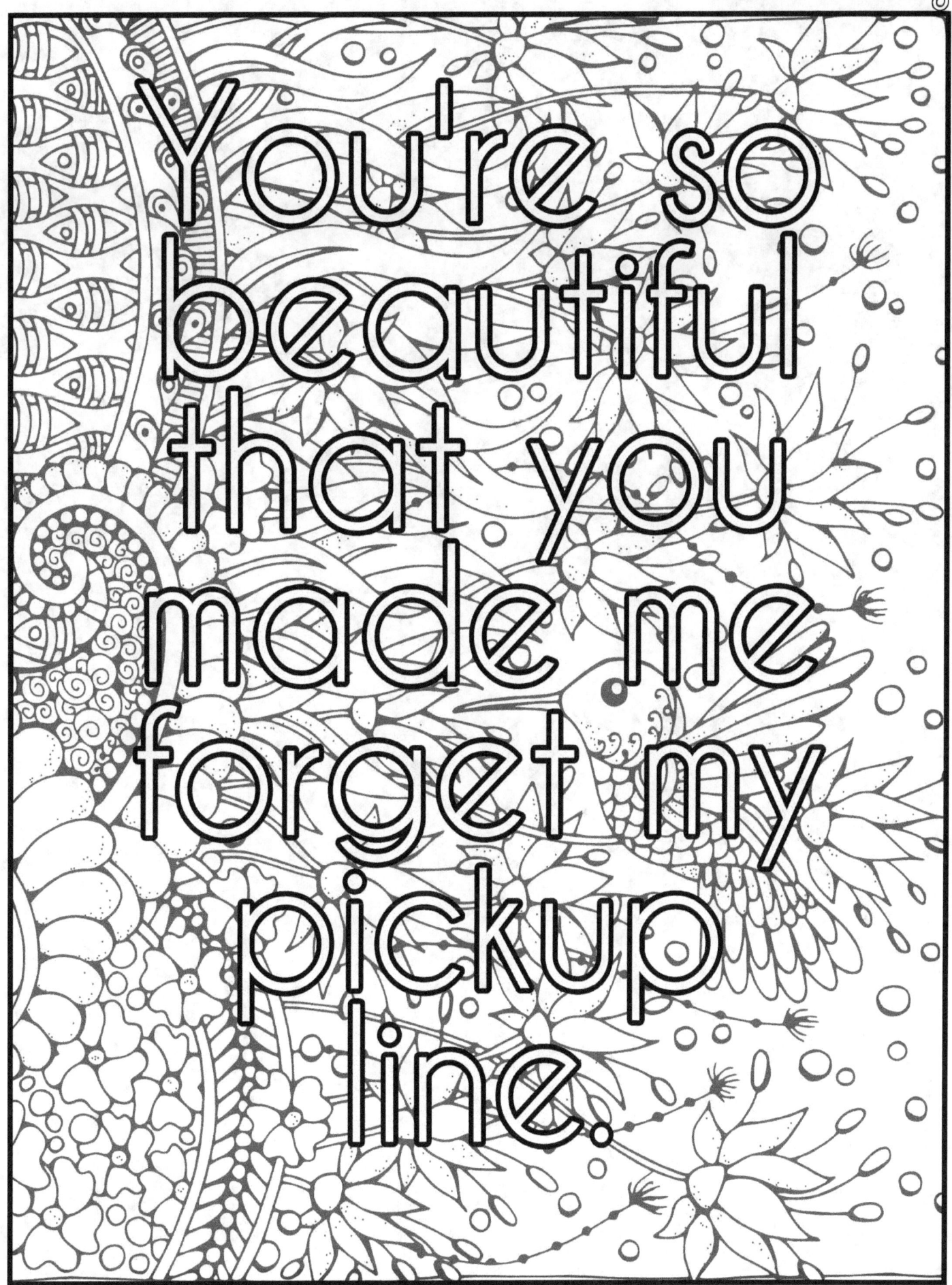

You're so beautiful that you made me forget my pickup line.

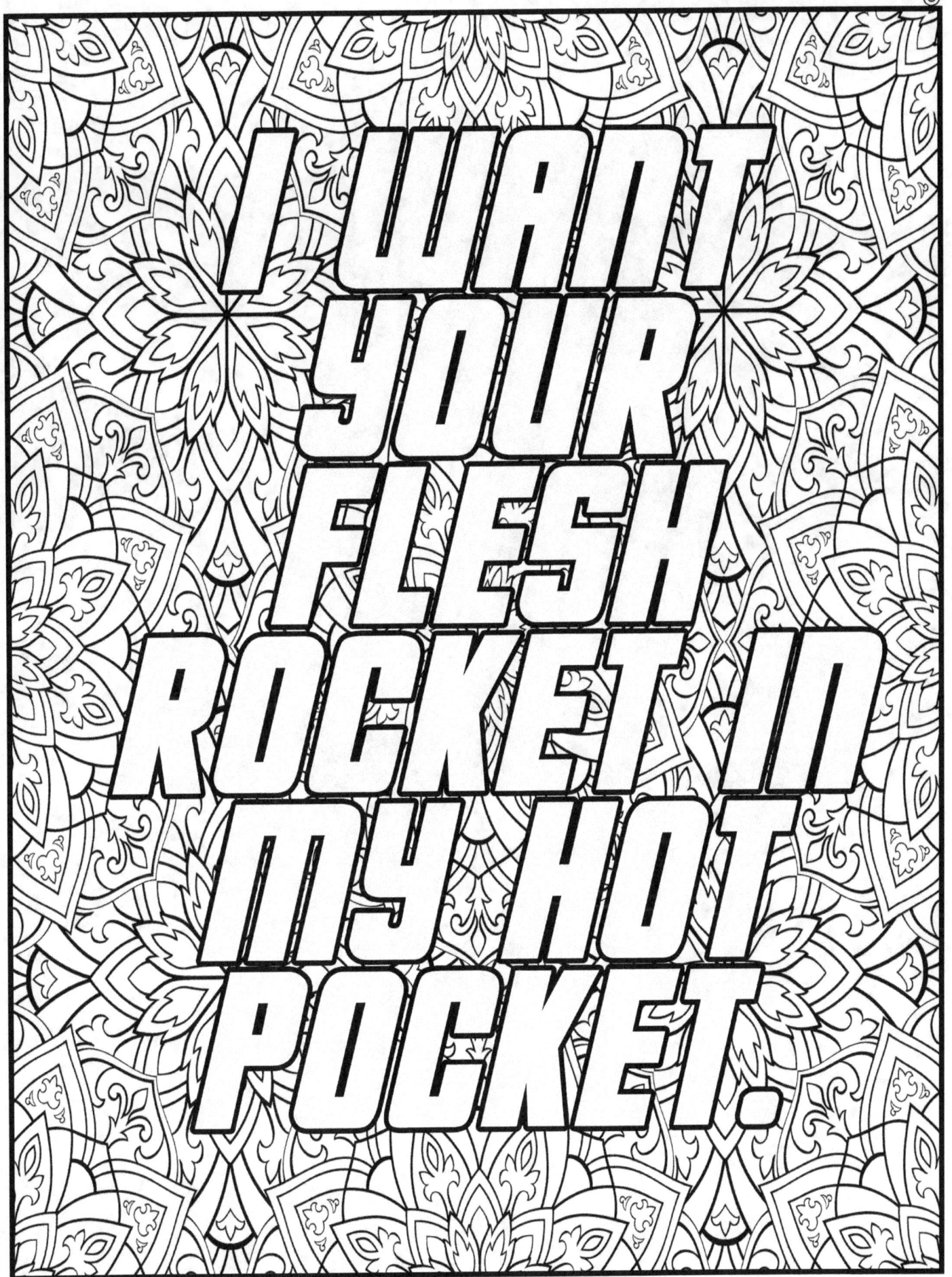

I WANT YOUR FLESH ROCKET IN MY HOT POCKET.

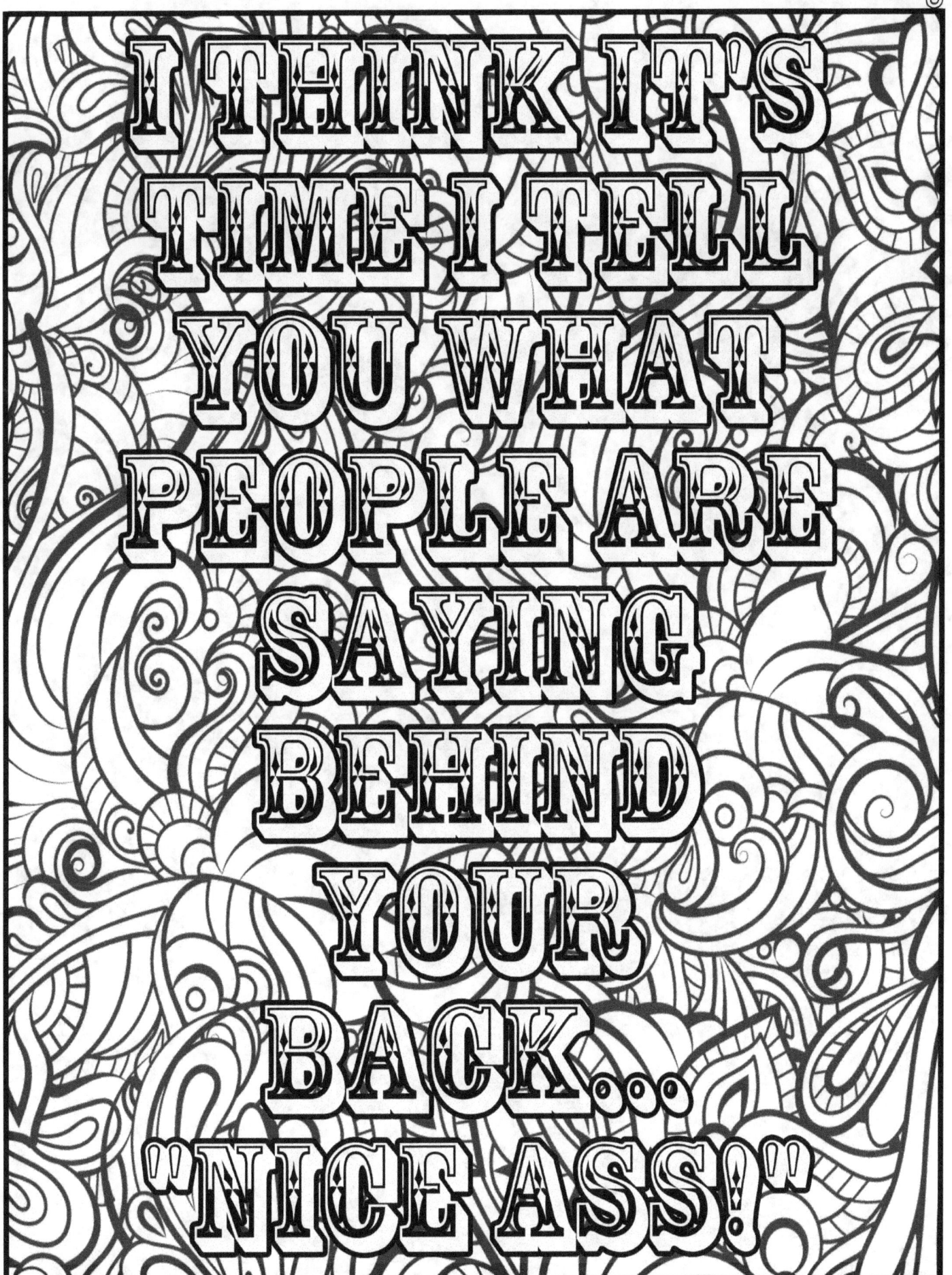

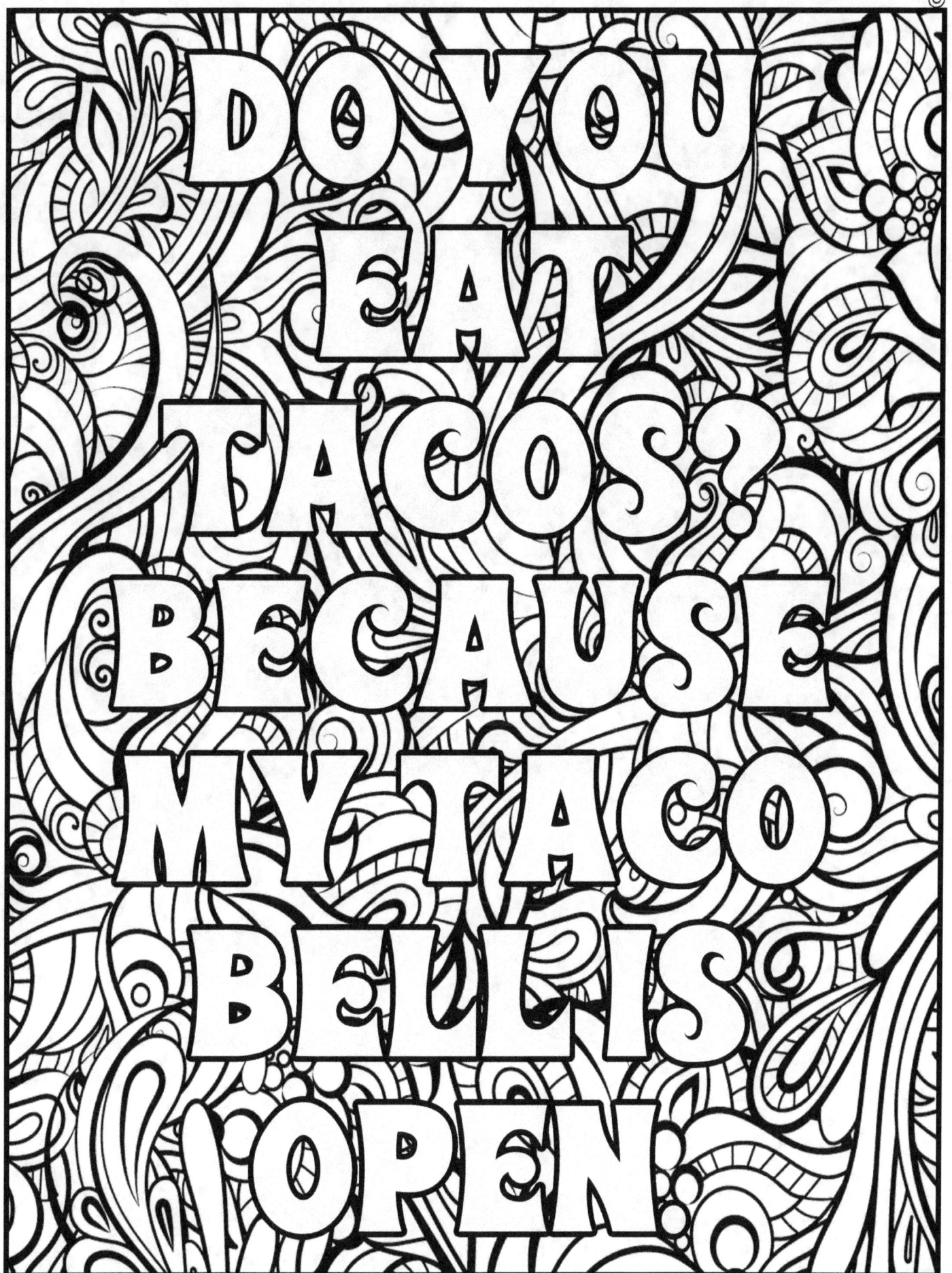

DO YOU EAT TACOS? BECAUSE MY TACO BELL IS OPEN

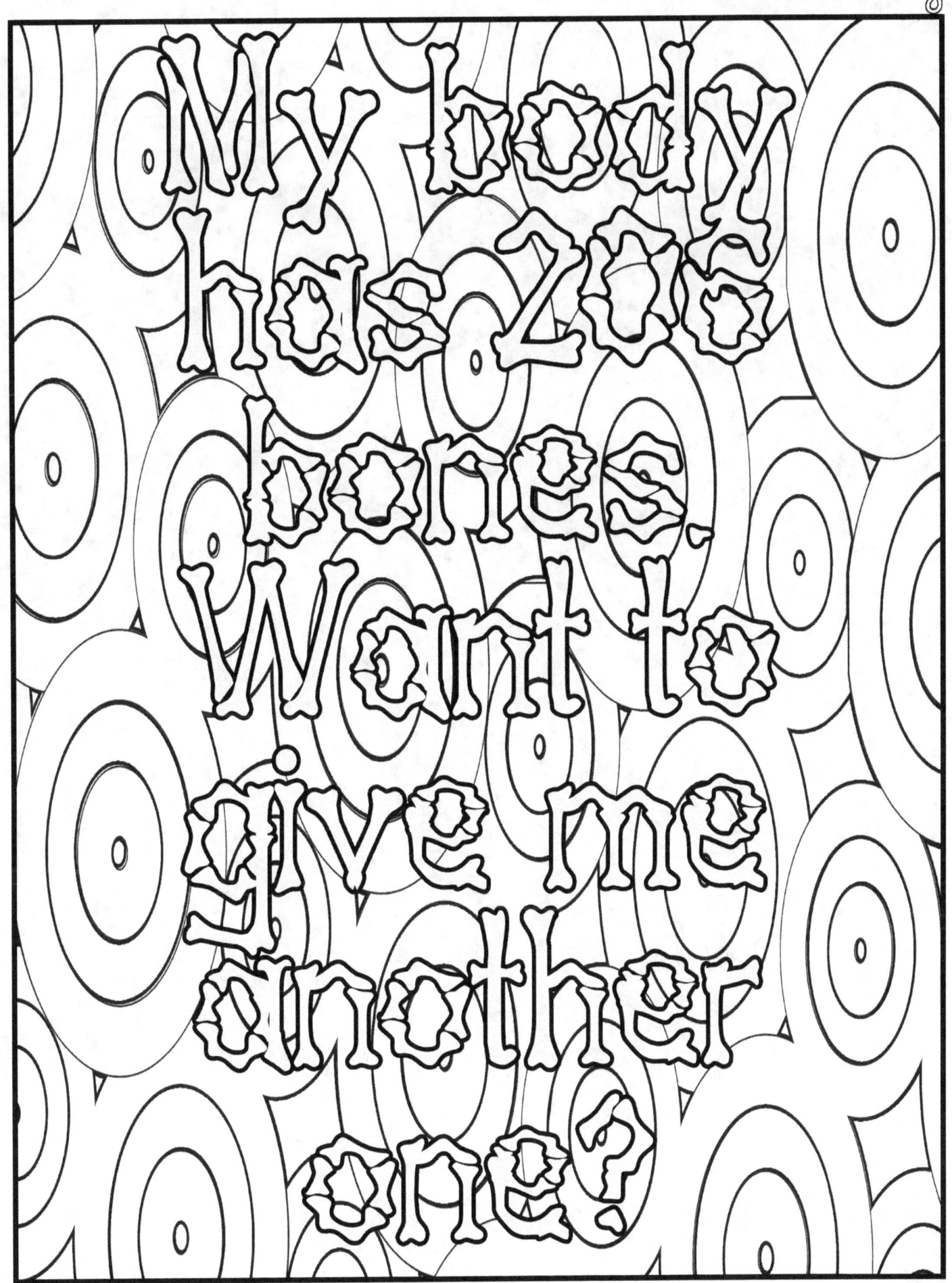

My body has 200 bones. Want to give me another one?

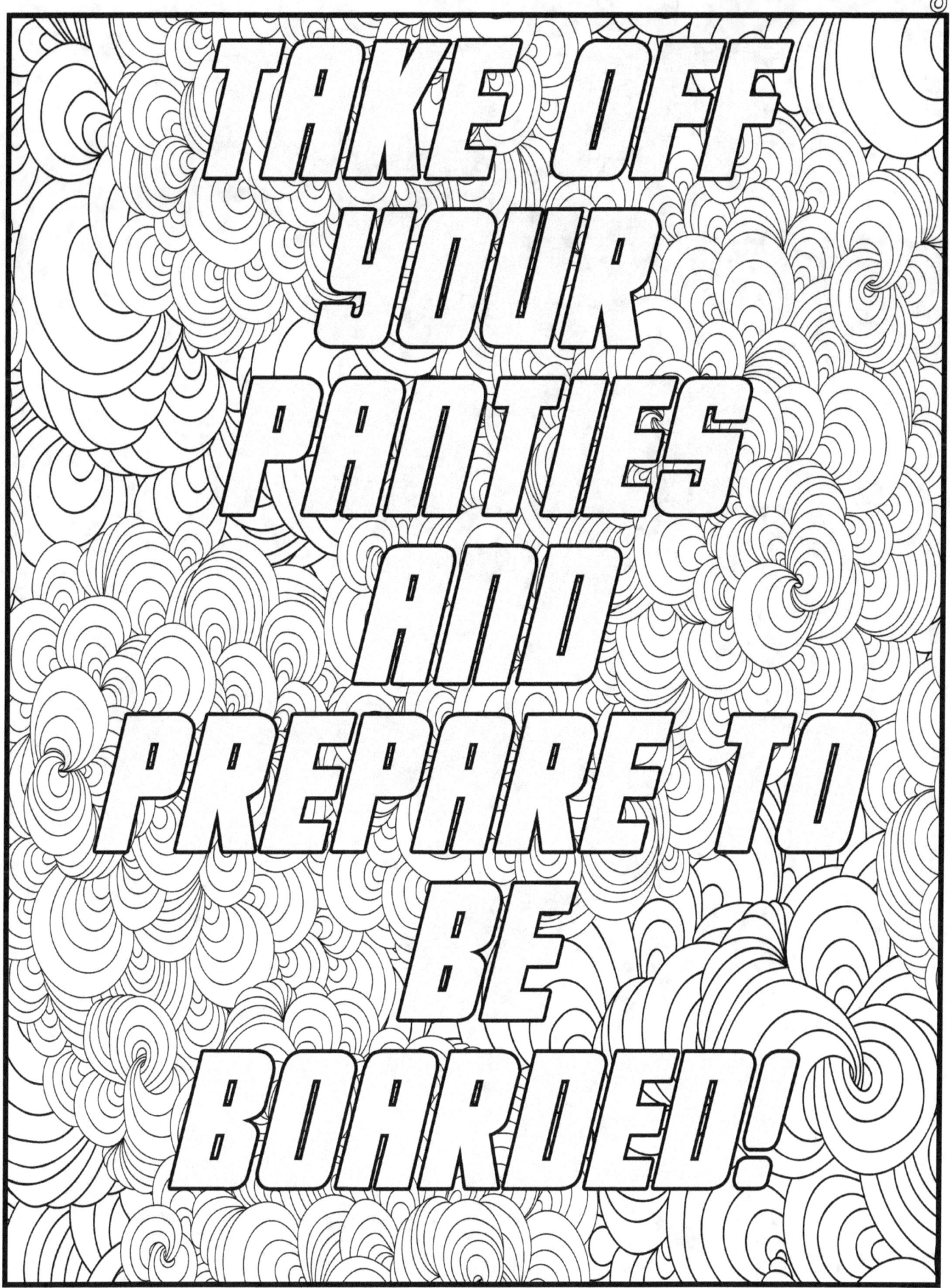

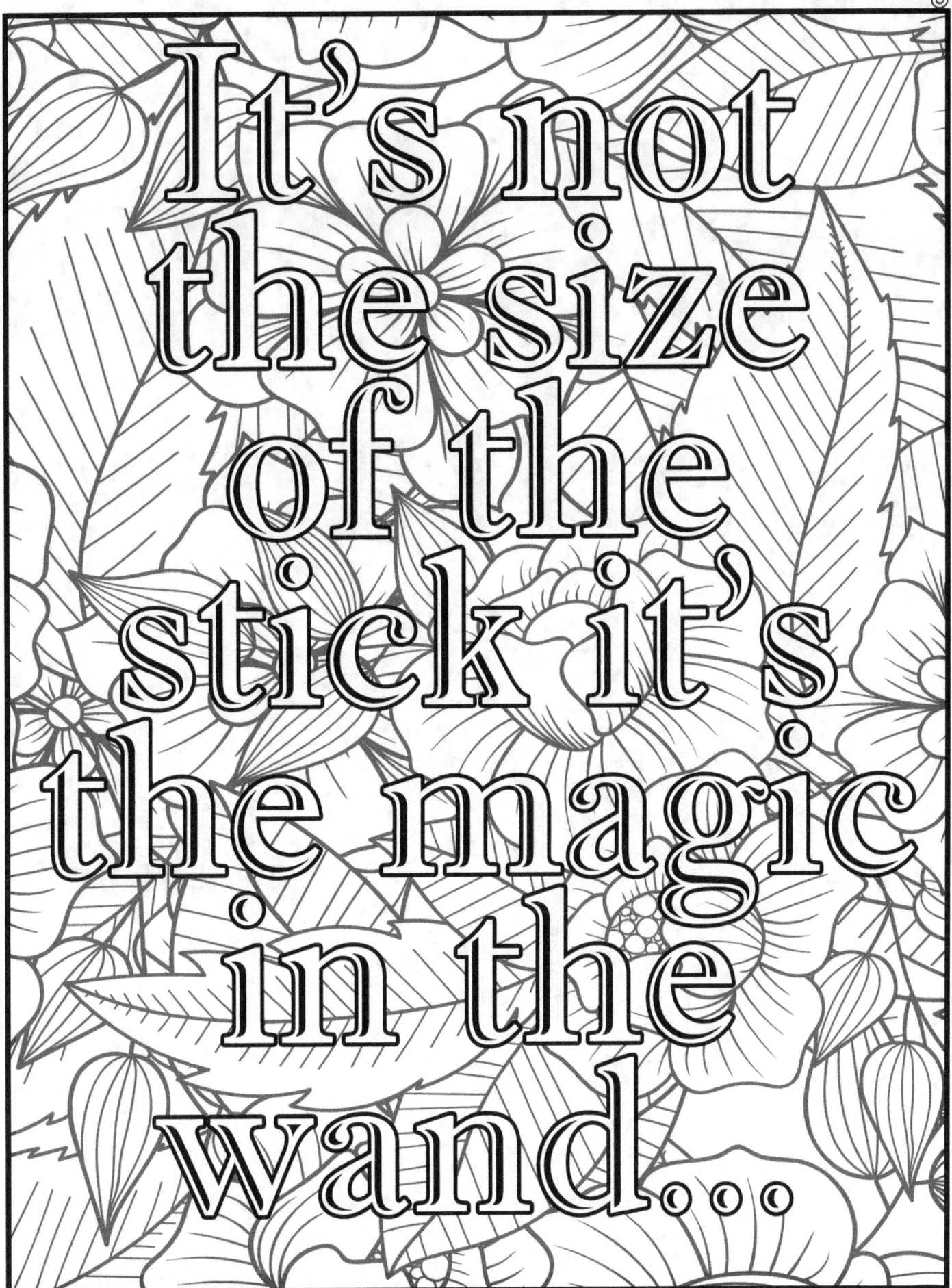

It's not the size of the stick it's the magic in the wand...

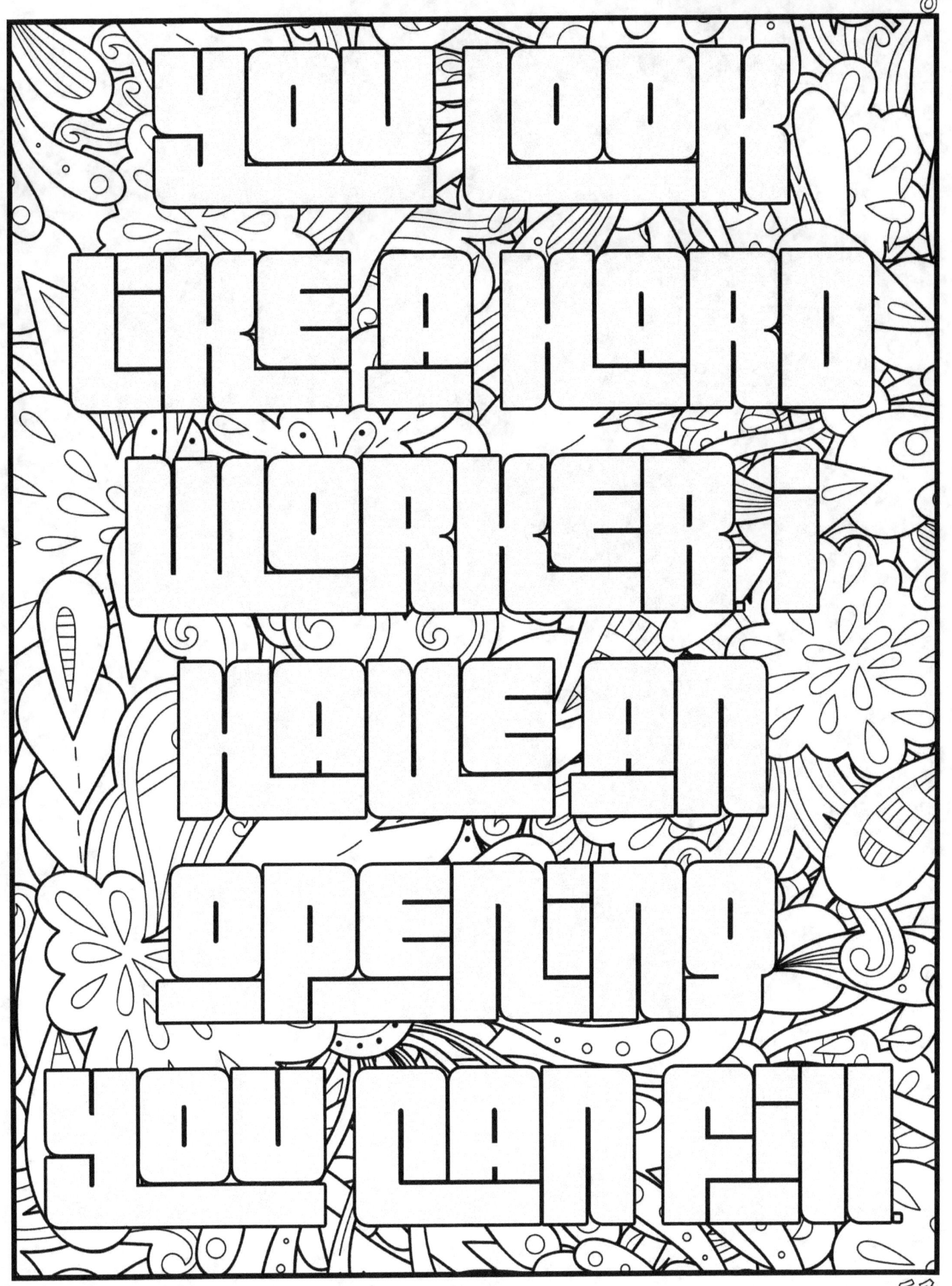

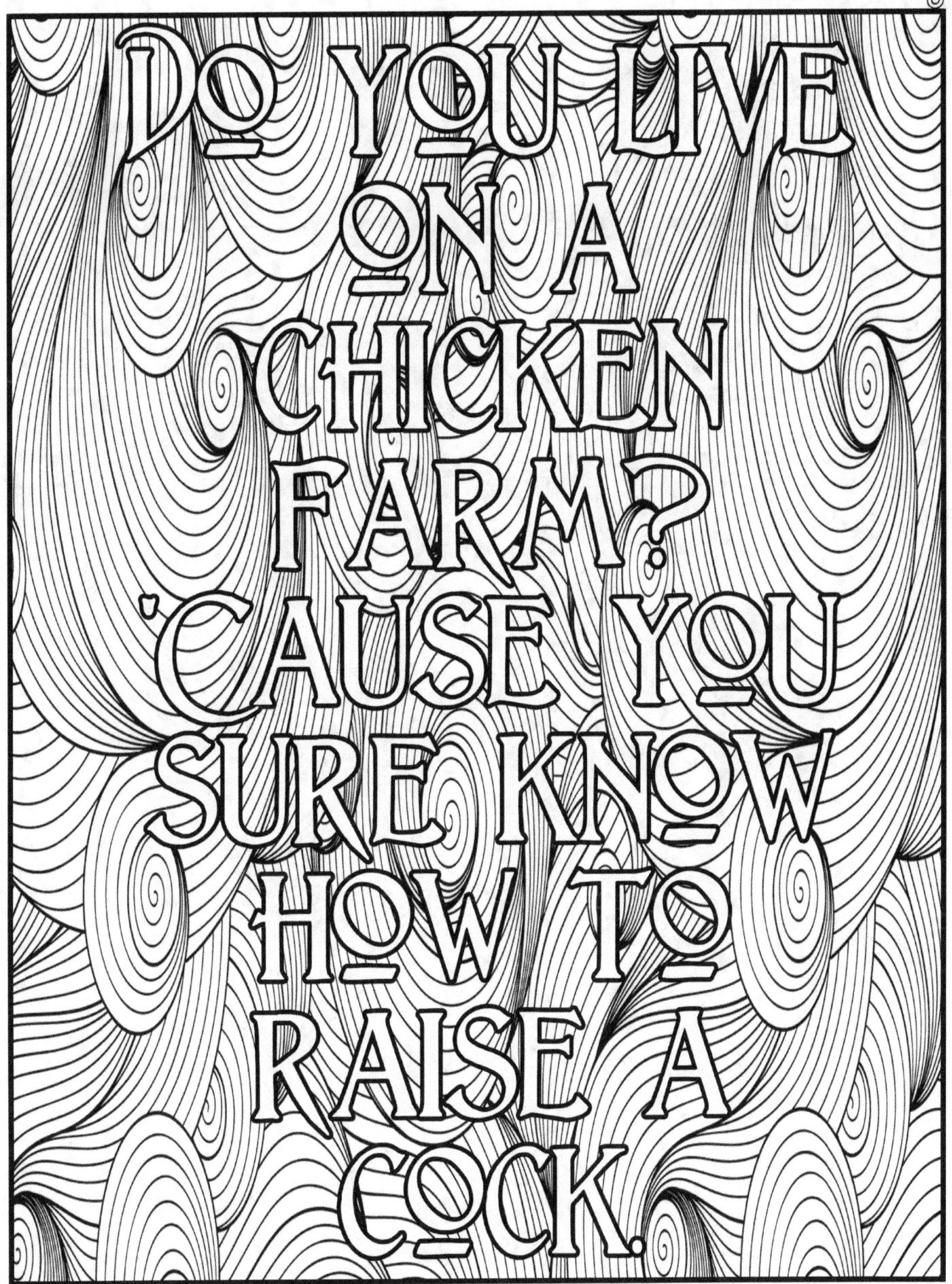

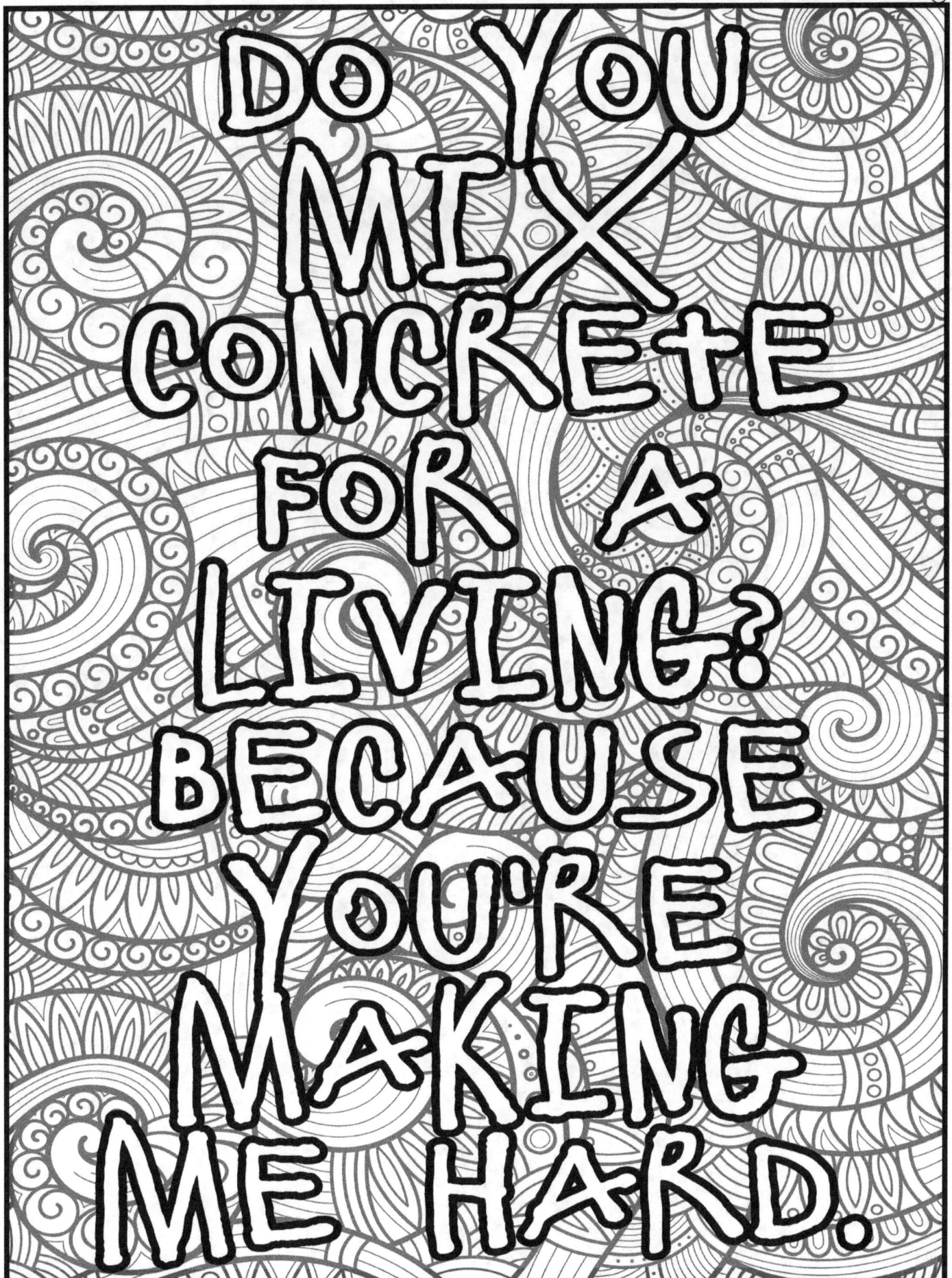

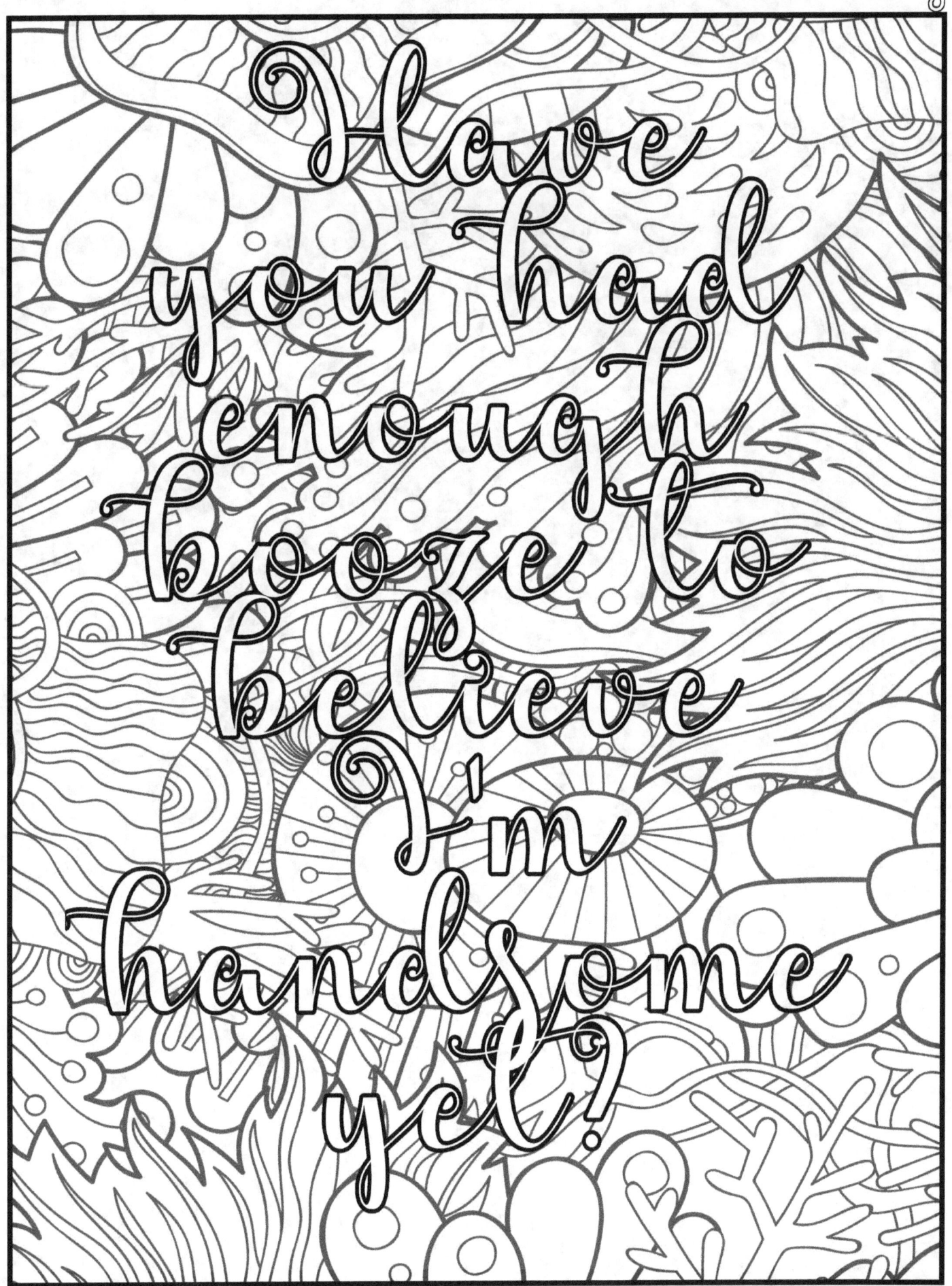

Have you had enough booze to believe I'm handsome yet?

www.ingramcontent.com/pod-product-compliance
Lightning Source LLC
Chambersburg PA
CBHW081254180526
45170CB00007B/2417